The Tales of Pate and Pip

By Joni Morton

I would like to dedicate this book to two

beautiful little girls.

Payton Marie and Piper LeeAnn Wiggins Aka

Pate and Pip.

My wish for you is to grow into beautiful women,

with beautiful hearts. May all your wishes come

true!

Thank you Katherine Ann Paxton for allowing

me

to feature your beautiful girls.

Pate and Pip

Introduction

Please take my hand and step under the foggy

Blue Mountains into the mystical land of Highwolf.

Highwolf is a beautiful land with beautiful people,

except one who is named Empusa. She is a beauty to

behold, long flaming hair, eyes the color of the sea,

bronze skin as soft as silk. However, it is not

Empusa's beauty to beware of, it is her nasty soul.

It is told throughout the land to beware of Empusa

for she will deceive anyone if she can gain anything

from them.

Let us begin our journey…

Once upon a time deep in the misty forest

lived a couple who had a daughter,

they named her Pate.

Oh, how they loved and worshipped

their beautiful child.

Pate grew up happy, with a heart as pure as gold.

She played in the misty forest and became friends

with many animals, even the beasts

of the forest loved Pate.

Through the years as she grew, so did her

beauty and many asked her to be their bride.

However, Pate was not interested; she knew in

her heart that when the right man came along,

she would feel it immediately. And she was in no

hurry

to leave. For she loved the little cottage her mother

made so homely, and her father took care of

with great pride, and she loved being with them.

One day as she lay daydreaming on soft grass

beside the Blue Mountains. She watched the birds fly

over and wondered where they might be off to on this

beautiful day. She was distracted by a noise and

looked up to see a handsome young man walking

out of the forest. As they saw each other, they were

both surprised. Pate asked him where he came

from and he said that he was just wondering around

looking at the beauty of the land, that it was not often

he got out.

He asked Pate what she was doing

and she told him

just wondering where the birds are going.

He asked if he may join her on the grass,

she told him yes

he may sit, so he sat and they began talking.

They talked of many things but after awhile

Pate told him that she must go, for surely her

parents would be getting worried. "Before you go

do you think we can meet again? I am sure I would

love to know if you find out where the birds may be

going." He asked.

Pate thought for only a moment then agreed

to meet him again.

Then as fast as her legs could run Pate ran home

to tell her parents about meeting the stranger.

They asked all kinds of questions that Pate had not

thought to ask. "Who is he, where does he come from,

who is his parents, what is his age?" She assured

them

they had agreed to meet again and she would be sure

to ask the questions, that they were curious about.

A few days later Pate went back to the stream,

and suddenly he was there. This time after a warm

greeting and asking if he may join her again,

Pate asked all the questions her parents wanted to

know.

He told of the magical land he came from

but for reasons only he knew, would not tell his

name.

However, it did not matter to Pate she enjoyed

his company, and did not think

it important to know everything.

They learned that they loved the same things,

and as the months passed they also learned they

loved each other.

And it was after this time, the Prince from

Castle hedge explained the reason for being mystical

about his identity and told Pate that he had to be sure

she didn't know who he was, for many far and

wide with selfish intentions wanted to be his bride.

He explained that he knew Pate's heart was

pure and that she loved his heart, not who he was.

And it was after this that he asked her father

if he could take his daughter to be his bride and

go to live with him in the Castle hedge Kingdom.

Pates parents knew the love between them and

agreed to let her marry. They had a beautiful

wedding

and people came from far and wide to give

blessing and wish a wonderful life together.

After days of celebrating, Pate packed her things,

kissed her parents goodbye and left the beautiful land

that she so loved.

Pate and her Prince

After Pate left her parents were very sad, they

no longer saw their beautiful daughter running

through the flowers beneath the misty mountains.

So one day they brought another life into their

home, another beautiful daughter, they called her Pip.

Pip was a free spirit, and a bit of a tomboy,

she loved life and everything in it. Her father

warned her constantly to not trust everyone,

for not all had the same heart as her. Pip took his

warnings with half heart and continued to live freely

without fear.

Some years later on a cold winter's night Pip's

father was very sick, and as he lay dying he made

Pip promise if she ever left home and met a beautiful

woman with green eyes, to return home

immediately, for she would not have Pips best

interest at heart.

After giving her promise, he told her goodbye

and then left to be with the angels. Pip was heart

broken

and missed her father terribly. For a very long

time she wasn't happy without her beloved father.

But time passed and Pip continued to grow

and learn, her mother taught her the things her father

no longer could.

She did the things her father used to do, like

shop in the village and while there, she met many

people who would say things she did not

understand.

They would say to her, "Aren't you lucky

to have a sister who is a queen!"

Pip would reply, "But I have no sister." Yet they

would

persist that she did indeed have a sister who was

Queen of the Castle hedge Kingdom, "your mother

just hasn't told you about her because she is

afraid that you will leave her too".

After hearing this for a very long time, early one

morning Pip asked her mother if she had a sister.

Her mother told her that indeed she did have a

sister that had married a prince a long time ago,

and had since became the Queen of the Castle

hedge Kingdom. Pip was amazed at this news

and was very curious.

She continued through the years, but always

wondered about the sister she never knew.

Pip

Early one morning she went to her mother and asked her permission to please let her go and meet her sister, until she could do nothing but allow her to go. But asked her to please swear that if she meets a beautiful woman with green eyes to return home immediately. It was then that Pip remembered her father making her swear to him this same promise many years before. And as Pip swore to her father, she also swore to her mother.

The next morning Pip set off on her way

and on her fourth day of travel she met a beautiful

woman with green eyes, so she went back home.

A few days later Pip set off again and after

traveling for 6 days she met the woman again,

but at this time Pip ignored her promise for she so

wanted to meet her sister she never knew.

The woman told Pip her name was Empusa and

asked Pip for hers.

Empusa

Pip replied, I am Pip from the land of Highwolf,

and carelessly said that she was on her way to the

Castle hedge Kingdom to meet

her sister who is the Queen.

Empusa told pip that she was

also on her way to

Castle hedge Kingdom and

said let us travel together.

So together, they traveled and

walked a very long way.

Pip became thirsty and Empusa

led her to a well of water,

which had neither rope nor pail. Empusa removed

her belt and told Pip she would lower her into the

well so she can drink. And so she did.

After Pip

had drank enough she shouted up to Empusa to

pull her out, but Empusa shouted down to Pip that

she will pull her out only if she promised that

from now on she would be the Queens sister.

Pip had no choice but to give

her promise. Empusa pulled

Pip from the well and they continued on their

way arriving there after two more days of walking.

Pate had news from her father many years before

that she had a sister, and it was always her wish to

one day meet her. After Empusa and Pip reached

the Kingdom's castle Pate received

her sister with much joy.

The next morning Empusa

offered Pate some entertainment,

I have with me a brave girl, and she will slay

anything, no matter what it is. Empusa wanted to get

rid of Pip because she was afraid

Pip would tell the truth.

"The mystical creature from the bottom of the sea

comes from time to time, maybe she can

slay it for me," Replied Pate. When Pip heard this

all she said was, "give me a fine stick from the

hardest tree, and lay a bonfire." Empusa prepared

everything, and Pip set out right away.

The sea creature

was attracted by the bonfire, approached Pip and

prepared to devour her. But Pip dealt it a deadly

blow to it's the head with her stick and slew it.

News spread that Pip slew the sea creature

and Pate awarded her a medal for she was fond

of the girl. Empusa was upset because she was

still afraid that Pip would tell Pate

that she was her real sister.

The next morning, Empusa asked Pate again if she

had any wishes, "yes" replied Pate. "As you go out

of Castle Hedge to the North there is a field of

honey, the sweetest in all the land. I send workers

there to collect it, but they never return.

The next morning Pip set out to the North taking

with her ninety soldiers. On their way, they came

upon a fellow sitting on the bank of a river that was

drinking all the water and spitting it out. Pip stopped

with the soldiers and watched, for she had never seen

anyone swallow so much water before. Finally,

she asked the fellow, "What are you doing?"

"There is nothing else I can do," he replied. "

"I just sit here all day and play with the water".

Then Pip asked him if he would like to come with her.

"Yes I would," the fellow said, and he

set out with Pip and her soldiers.

They continued on their way

North and came upon

another fellow playing with some rabbits. He would

catch them; let them go, then catch them again.

Pip asked the fellow what he was doing and

he replied, "There's nothing else I can do but catch

rabbits all day."

Pip told him they are on their way north in search

of the sweetest honey in all the land, and would

he like to join them. "Yes indeed," he replied

and they all set off again.

After riding for a long time, they sat down under

an oak tree to rest. In the tree was a nest of baby birds,

a snake was creeping up the tree to devour them.

When Pip saw this, she reached into her bag,

took her hard stick, and slew the snake.

At that very moment the mother bird arrived,

it set upon Pip and tried to gouge out her eyes,

but the baby birds cried out, "No, no she saved

us from the snake!" The mother

bird asked Pip, "You saved

my children from the snake, what I can do for you?"

But Pip told the bird there was nothing she wanted,

so the mother bird plucked out a feather from its

wing and said, "take this feather and if you ever

need me, burn it and I will come

to your aid right away.

Pip took the feather and put it in her bag, and the

group set off North again.

Going North

On their way, they came upon

an anthill. They went

around it, taking care not to step on it. The queen

of the ants asked, "Why did you

not step on the ant hill?"

"I did not want to do you any harm," replied Pip.

The ant queen declared, "You have done us a great

service, and as thanks I will

give you one of my wings.

If you ever are in need of help burn it and I will

come to your aid with all of my army right away."

Pip thanked the ant queen and they continued north.

They traveled one more day then arrived where

the entire land was covered with delicious honey.

As they entered, the army from the village of

Northbridge met them. Pip informed the leader

that they were there to collect honey for

Queen Pate that lives in the land of Castle hedge.

The land of honey

The leader retorted, "If you can eat three hundred plates of food, you can take the honey". The fellow who had drunk all the water from the river said he was willing to try. The leader sent for three hundred plates of food, and the fellow ate them all. The leader became worried then said, "whoever wins the flag in a race with my swiftest horses can have the honey." the young man who had been catching the rabbits told Pip to not worry that indeed he would be the winner of the race. The man told the riders "I will give you one head start."

The horses galloped away,

and then the rabbit catcher set out at last, caught

up with them, passed them, and won the flag.

After this, the leader was more worried,

but still would not give up the honey.

Then he came up with a mighty

idea and said, "I have a

barn full of wheat, barley, and oats all mixed

together, you must sort them all out for me in three

days and if you do not, we keep the honey."

Now Pip was feeling despaired because she knew

it was impossible to sort out that much grain in

three days. Then she remembered the ant's wing

and threw it into a fire.

Immediately the queen of

the ants arrived and asked Pip what she wanted. Pip

told the queen about the grains, so the queen

summoned her ant army. And in three hours, the

grain was separated into three piles. Then Pip said to

the leader, "now you must give us the honey!"

The leader just could not believe Pip had sorted the

grain and had to see it with his own eyes, and to

his amazement, the grain was

indeed sorted into three piles.

Then the leader told Pip, "I have one more request,

I want you to bring me a bottle of water from the

mountains whose peaks touch. At the bottom of

these mountains is a cave and inside this cave is

the water you must bring to me. This water is a

remedy to bring the dead back to life."

Pip remembers the bird's feather

and threw it into the fire.

The bird appeared and asked Pip what is her desire.

Pip told the bird about the water she needed from the

mountains whose peaks touch. At once, the bird flew

away and in no time, it brought

Pip the bottle of water,

which Pip presented to the leader.

The leader and his soldiers stepped aside,

Pip and her army gathered

all the honey they could carry and together

made their way back to the castle.

They were singing and laughing when they

arrived and Empusa heard this

and went out to meet them.

When she saw Pip had returned safe and

sound with the honey she was furious!

And in her anger, she drew her sword and chopped

Pip in two. When Pate found out Empusa had slain

Pip of whom she was fond, she was so upset she

could not eat nor sleep. Even though she did not

punish Empusa, because she believes her to be

her sister, she refused to see her or anyone anymore.

Meanwhile one of the soldiers sprinkled the water

from the cave over Pip and brought her back to life.

The next morning Pip went to the castle and said, "I

am here

to see Queen Pate!" However, the servants said she

cannot see the Queen because she is in mourning and

would not see anyone. Nevertheless, Pip insisted,

so they sent a message to Pate telling her there is a

youth there insisting to her. Pate told them to let her

in,

when Pip arrived in the Queens chamber she began

asking Pate, "If someone makes a promise and has

been cut in two she can't come back to life can she?"

"No," said Pate, "she can't come back to life".

Then Pip asked, "If she is cut in two and then does

come back to life is she still

bound to keep her promise?"

"No, no one is bound by a promise after his or

her death." said Pate.

"Fine said Pip, now I can tell you what I couldn't

before, for I have died then returned back to life,

I can tell you that it is I who is your real sister.

The other is a deceiver who I promised that I

would never say anything as long as I lived."

Then Pip told Pate everything

that happened on her journey.

Pate was overjoyed and embraced Pip, and a

great feast was held.

Then Pate ordered a great

stove to be fired and Empusa thrown into it so

she could never deceive another, and so it was

done. The two sisters were so happy being

together they sent for their mother and all lived

happily ever after in Castle Hedge Kingdom.

Then end…

Dear reader I greatly appreciate you for reading

The Tales of Pate and Pip. Please take a moment

to rate my book, and if you would like, leave a

review.

You can also find my other work at this address.

amazon.com/author/jonimorton